Into the Adirondacks

Jim Poulette

North Country Books
Utica, New York

On the cover: Algonquin Peak from near the Wright junction.

Into the Adirondacks

Some of the material in this book has been published previously in Adirondac, the magazine of the Adirondack Mountain Club, and Adirondack Peeks, the magazine of the Adirondack 46ers. Both of these organizations advocate a peaceful coexistance with the Adirondack Forest Preserve.

PRINTED IN THE UNITED STATES OF AMERICA.
10 9 8 7 6 5 4 3 2 1
PRINTED ON RECYCLED PAPER.

North Country Books, Inc., Publisher - Distributor
18 Irving Place, Utica, New York, 13501-5618

Library of Congress Cataloging-in-Publication Data

for Mom & Dad

Contents

Forward

These stories are about mountains and people. I'm not sure why but for some reason I have always equated the mountains with the forces of good in the world, or maybe God, or whatever it is that encourages us to feel good about ourselves. Writing about spiritual events in my life is very difficult for me. It probably came from something in my childhood that never defined what spiritualism really was. I have always had my fair share of conventional as well as unconventional religion. But it still took all these years and all these mountains to teach me the difference between religion and spiritualism. An old mountain climbing friend once told me that spiritualism didn't really need religion. Its been hard for me to forget those words. If these events and people that I were to write about were fictional it may have been somewhat different. I could make happy endings in every story and make every character fearless and indefatigable. But in reality sometimes the mountains can conjure fear and the forest and the valleys and the rivers can at times seem hostile. I think that I have always been here, coexisting with this fear, and at times becoming a part of it. One thing that remains constant, the best days of my life have been spent in these mountains and wilderness areas of the Adirondacks with friends and family and sometimes with no one at all.

The following pages represent a collection of notes and short stories written while I was in the process of completing the requirements for membership in a climbing society known as the Adirondack Forty-Sixers. These notes also contain some of my personal opinions about the people, organizations, and the ethical circumstances that I have encountered while in the Adirondacks. Some of these views you may or may not agree with but I hope that in the end you will at least have thought about some of the more important issues that confront today's wilderness.

The only requirement for membership in the Forty-Sixers is essentially climbing the forty six highest mountains in New York State. At the time it didn't really sound like that much of a task and I thought that I might even enjoy some aspects of this itinerary. For years I had admired the conservation oriented principals and creed of the Forty-Sixers. Years ago while in the Boy Scouts my troop and I had volunteered for trail work and they all seemed like very environmentally sensitive people and just good folks. Even though I didn't really like the thought of mountain climbing or camping in bear infested woods or any of that kind of stuff it just didn't seem to matter all that much. Getting to know the mountains just seemed like a healthy, appropriate, and noble thing to do at the time.

I recall it as being late August 1966. It was my first ascent of an Adirondack high peak and I will never forget that experience. I recall it as an ascent as long as you don't mind the definition as being virtually coaxed and dragged to the summit by your father. Of course it had to be Mt. Marcy and of course the approach had to be via Lake Colden, the miserable mile, and Four Corners lean-to. A longer distance between two points I will never know. At the time I was all of nine years old and my brother, who I truly believed was the only other one who knew what I was going through, was younger then I was. My feet were covered with blisters and my boots were soaking wet. I was hungry, thirsty, tired, hyperthermic, muddy, bug-bitten, and quite tired of this whole concept of mountain climbing. To this day I will never understand how we made it to the summit. How we overcame the rain, the fog, the blackflies, the muddy trails, and the steep rocks was beyond my imagination. I don't know how we did it but we did it. The lean-to at Four Corners is long gone now. In the passing years

9

since I was to relive that climb a thousand times. To this day whenever I'm moved to throw my pack in the car and go 'climb Marcy' I am usually blessed by the sight of first time ascenders struggling to reach the top of an obstacle which at a distance must seem very impossible. I would also have the great fortune to relive this experience through my own son while accompanying him on his first high peak ascent. It was Phelps in winter. Sure he got through it alright and at times he even acted like he was enjoying himself. But I knew that, like myself years ago, it was too early for him to thirst for the adversity that the mountains would challenge him with. He would be back when he was ready.

When he does comes back things will not be the same. Change is coming in a big way to the Adirondacks. Lean-to's are being removed, camping areas are disappearing. There's talk of a ban on campfires, and user permits, and huge shopping center like parking facilities. Everybody is scared, landowners, users, government, everybody. What should we do? I'm not really sure, are you.

Twenty years after my first Marcy ascent came the inspiration and drive to pursue and complete the climbing of the forty-six high peaks. With this inspiration came friendships, experiences, and an education in the nature of the mountains, as well as the true meaning of my own spiritualism, that I would not have otherwise had the opportunity to gain. Hopefully my son and daughter who at this time in their lives are a bit preoccupied with "mall life" and music television and thinks that the mountains are "kind of boring", will over time come to see what the peaks can do for them. Someday they will have the chance to be caught on a high peak in a snowstorm, or in a valley during a thunderstorm, or feel the power of a nearby landslide, or follow a brook to its very origin, and feel comfortable and at home surrounded by what nature has to offer. I think they will love it.

To those who can relate to the kind of peace and friendly familiarity that the wilderness and the mountains can provide, these stories are for you.

Meeting Grace

As I walked down the wooden steps toward Boulders, on my way to finally meeting Grace L. Hudowalski the Forty Sixer Historian, the atmosphere that surrounded the camp and the hemlock and cedar forest that stood before me was breathtaking. Nestled on the western shore of Schroon Lake in a small town called Adirondack, New York, was a shrine to the very existence of the Adirondack Mountains, and the summer home and Forty-Sixer headquarters of the much talked about and written about "Grace". She appeared from behind the screen door, a sturdy blond haired lady whose years had been kind indeed, and after I had introduced myself it was if we had known each other for years. For in reality we did know each other through the many letters I had written to her and the many years that carried me through the climbing of the forty six peaks. Grace was certainly one of the reasons that I continued to climb in the Adirondacks.

When I entered the camp at Boulders it was if I was entering another world where climbing is part of daily life, and letters describing various trials and tribulations in the mountains were everywhere. The walls of the cabin were covered with photographs and paintings of mountain after mountain. It was a place of nobility and permanence.

As we sat in the front room drinking fresh hot orange mint tea, picked fresh from near her home in Albany, she gave me a tour through her weeks mail. Letters from all over the United States could be seen, people beginning, people finishing, and people just writing to tell their special story. She walked me through the camp which was filled with memorabilia of the Adirondacks as well as pictures of herself and of her deceased husband Ed Hudowalski. As a team Grace and Ed were to begin and personify the exploration of the Adirondack mountains and wilderness areas.

Her stories were wonderfully endless. She told me about the Marshalls and Herb Clark, the early explorers of this mainly unchartered region. She told me about Esther Macomb, the hitch-ups, Noah Rondeau the hermit and mayor of Cold River New York, and the great landslide that carved and exposed the cliffs and dike that we now recognize as Mt. Colden. She told me about Henry Van Hoevenburg and his dream for what now is called the Adirondack Loj - and the circumstances behind its unique spelling. She told me these stories with an authority that only eighty years experiencing and living the Adirondacks could bring.

Through the years, and as the popularity of the high peaks grew, I was to have the good fortune to assist Grace in helping to answer the onslaught of mail that she received. Thousands of people were writing the Forty-Sixers every year reporting their adventures in the mountains. My feelings about this situation were and continue to be very mixed. Were the canisters placed on the untrailed summits actually attracting more wilderness users. Were the herd paths worn out by these thousands of climbers, and the erosion and deterioration of the wilderness setting, really in the best interest of the mountains. Grace explains that people will climb these mountains anyway and as long as they are they might as well record their experiences for future generation. Her favorite response to me was "You can't stop the recording of history - no matter what it's about". It's hard to argue.

People get upset when 46ers talk about the possibility of dismantling the canisters maintained by the club on the untrailed summits and marking trails. They say that the 46ers, or anyone else, do not have the right to deny them the same opportunities for recreation and adventure in the mountains. They speak as if the experience were the same as it was when Grace was climbing. Hardly. In the next decade the questions will have to be answered.

And still the letters come by the hundreds and by the thousands. And still Grace answers them, in one way or another, by the hundred and by the thousand. She continues to be an amazing 46er. Thanks for answering my letters Grace.

The snow conditions during the walk in were marginal and we all chose to wear snowshoes upon reaching the first bridged river crossing. This was an old iron suspension bridge and was both snow covered and quite shaky. Even though the darkness hid the river the haunting sound of the ice filled water kept you well informed of its presence. The crossing was uneventful and passed quickly. Further on toward Lake Sally the snow had a crusty layer of ice from the warm conditions and the dark silence of the early morning was broken only by our aluminum snowshoes scratching and clawing at the trail. Occasionally the light mumbles of conversation between group members would intervene. The warm unseasonable air had me sweating and within twenty minutes we stopped to shed our pile jackets. Already most in the group were down to a single layer of poly and everyone continuously commented on the spring like conditions. Certainly odd for winter. Stan, Paula, and I, chose to keep on our gore-tex bib overalls. It appeared that the three of us were not getting the workout that the others were on the approach. It began sleeting lightly. Seven headlamp beams pointed downward jittering through out the trail which was cut out from dense pines on either side. The reflections being made from the snow laden trees as well as the reflective trail gave our route an almost tunnel like appearance. Again Paula filled the void of silence, "I wish there was a way that I could take some of this home with me". I knew she was talking about her photography. These kind of experiences were hard to document and she was quickly learning this. It always made me wonder how people always tried to store these kind of spiritual events in these small boxes. I stopped carrying a camera years ago. Tiny hail like ice crystals bounced off our packs and made tinkling sounds like a hundred tiny bells. The darkness was cold and silent, it was the dawn of a new winter in this dismal wilderness called the Adirondacks.

After an hour of steady snowshoeing we came upon the large suspension bridge crossing the Opalacent River. It was a raging torrent of water and we could barely hear each other over its loud roar. Ignoring both the bridge and the trail Stan continued down to the waters edge and began snowshoeing down stream. Puzzled I yelled, "Where in the hell are you going". The rivers drone covered all sounds so I quickly ran down to join him. "What's going on", watching him remove a shank of rope from his pack. "God forbid if anyone should fall in I'll have a rope ready to snag them - now go get everyone across", he yelled over the river. His headlamp shining in my eyes told me he was in no mood for an argument. I turned quickly and snowshoed back up to where the group was waiting. My mind couldn't help but go back two years ago to a winter ascent of the trailless peaks Street and Nye. On the return the leader, probing the ice on Indian Pass Brook for a safe crossing point, fell through into chest high water. The sights and sounds of pulling him out of the raging water, his snowshoes and backpack like blocks of ice. The yelling of group members trying desperately to remove his clothing before they froze to his body.

"What's going on?" Paula's headlamp illuminated the trail between us. "Is everything OK?" Rejoining the group I explained Stan's plan and we all moved toward the crossing. One by one we inched our way across the swinging walkway which dipped down in the center to within several feet of the river. Huge ice spears hung from the bridge and dangled into the water creating even more turbulence and making the walkway ice covered at the bottom. The steel cables supporting the bridge moaned and creaked as we all crossed. Soon we were safely on the east side of the river. We watched in silence as Stan and his lone light climbed back up to the trail and then finally crossed the bridge. The light from his lamp vibrated as he crossed and it highlighted the warm steam coming from his breathing. His laughter broke the roar of the river and he told us the story of how last year a group from Albany, during an ill - fated attempt of Allen, came upon the river only to find that the bridge had been destroyed by ice coming down stream. "They were like ants", he shouted. "They ran up and down the bank for hours trying to find a safe place to cross. By the time they finally realized it was hopeless I was back in my truck drinking coffee". His laughter echoed off the surrounding hills. He was such a remarkable fellow and I have yet to figure the extent of his love for the Adirondacks on this his tenth winter ascent of Allen Mountain.

Shepherd's Tooth

As Paula and I relaxed and laid back on the small summit of this bushwhack nightmare, I thought about feeling good. I thought about how wonderful the wind felt and sounded as the silence absorbed us. We all have special places, pastimes, and people that make us feel good. These are the places and people that we want to connect with because they reflect back to us who and what we really are. Many people get closer to themselves, to their instinctual inner knowing, when surrounded by the earth's natural elements. Shepherd's Tooth was our place.

Most of us have an inner yearning to connect with nature to rebuild our relationship with her. Whether it has something to do with a collective consciousness formed millions of years ago or just a modern way of healing from the stress of congested twentieth century living, we all do it. We all seek that mutual datum that only nature and the halls of the forest can provide. When we reach those points in our lives where we have had enough of the florescent lights, instant food, and instant entertainment, we inevitably turn to the earth with its infinite wonders. It rarely lets us down.

We lay here loving the wilderness. We lay here loving these mountains and thinking that it could never have been any other way. Occasionally we volunteer for trail maintenance work to give something back and to return some of the balance to this fragile alpine environment. Through the years we have found that our appreciation of, and connection with these elements in nature, has nurtured our own relationship. It has acted as our board room, mediator, grievance department, creative stage, sounding board, easy chair, and of course health club. We brainstorm here. We make major decisions here. We meet with family and friends here. It seems for me to be the most comfortable place for creativity and clear thinking. From the distance and height above the treeline we gain perspective on our lives and return with a clearer sense of what is important.

Why do we love these crazy trailless peaks? These mountains do not have marked trails - we could get lost. During the summer months informal herd paths beaten out by many hikers through the years can aid a person in finding these untrailed peaks. During the autumn and winter months however, when leaves and snow hide these paths, these routes become a real challenge. At these times a map and compass are used to navigate to the intended destination in a new game called orienteering.

On occasion we encounter rain, snow, mud or, wind and at times the untimely occurrence of nightfall. On one memorable hike with sisters from a local convent it took us nine hours to make the summit of Couchsachraga. We arrived back at our cars around midnight. Hungry and exhausted, but all the better for the experience, we left the adversity of that day and went back to our respective lives. Climbing that mountain, much like this one, represented a major achievement that was ours. I think of that day often. I will think of this day in much the same way.

Feeling good in the mountains is not a new concept although on Shepherd's Tooth you may be pushing the experience. Some believe that the wilderness can be an appropriate environment for recognizing, understanding, and laying the groundwork for solving the problems that come and go in our lives. These mountains excersize all of our emotions and allow them to come to the surface. Some of these emotions may stem from the challenges presented during the climb, but they normally go much deeper then that. Frustration, anger, fear, joy, wonder, sadness - all of these have come out today, pulled to the surface by the beauty and adversity of this little mountain. This feeling is that of feeling the full range of emotions and of knowing that occurrence and time are in harmony here. I remember reading the teachings of an eastern philosopher, he said:" To be happy in nature and comfortable with its divine order, and to understand that we are a unique and interconnected part of the entire living world system, is the highest wisdom that we could ever hope to achieve". Hopefully in time the people in this world will be able to appreciate all of this enough to want to protect it so that it will last forever.

As I look down toward Indian Pass two hawks circle above Iroquois. Their faint screams fight to be heard above the whisper of the wind. The little pine tree rocks back and forth to the gentle rhythm of the breeze. The sun is warm on my face. Paula is asleep now. I think I will sleep, for awhile.

The Story of Cliff and Redfield

Once upon a time there was a dauntless band of backpackers destined for Cliff and Redfield. They gathered from far and wide and brought greetings from such far away places as St. Regis Falls, Malone, Pittsburg, and of course Glens Falls. They hoisted giant packs and began the long trek to Lake Arnold. Along the way they battled hungry chickadees near Marcy Dam and avoided giant immovable toads near Avalanche Camps. Nearing the Mt. Colden junction five hearty group members, led by an intrepid climber and dining companion, decided to climb Colden while the remainder made their way down toward Uphill lean-to. The hike to Feldspar brought out the Tom Sawyer in everyone as they hopped from floating plank to floating plank at the base of the new Colden land slide. The new slide with its newly carved waterfalls raging was quite a sight. Arriving at Uphill the light showers subsided, tents were set up, and preparations were made to ascend Redfield. The brook roared with power never seen by anyone who had climbed here before and on the upper sections the conditions were not unlike that of South American waterfall climbing. The fearless couple from Pittsburg found the canister, and all in all the climb took three hours round trip from Uphill, very respectable for a group this size.

Later that evening while everyone was crawling into sleeping bags the group was the first to receive information from another climbing party that they had lost a climber in the dark on Cliff hours earlier. After a short meeting and the decision for a full night of sleep, first light sunday morning found our group and the lost hikers brother assembled to ascend Cliff and hopefully establish contact with the lost hiker. Nearing the brook cairn on the steep pitch, and after much calling out by the group, the intrepid climber was the first to hear the lost hikers call for help. He and the brother separated from the group, found the lost hiker, and eventually brought him back down to Uphill Lean-to where a DEC representative was waiting to complete a report as well as call off a potential search party. Quite a feat of search and rescue expertise even for the intrepid climber. The moral of that story has not changed: keep a hiking group together, carry gear to expect a bivouac, and if you do get lost - stay put! This hiker had only the clothes on his back and was stumbling in the exact opposite direction toward Tahawus.

Rejoice was the call from Cliff, and after

some weird altimeter readings showing that the true summit of Cliff may still be up for grabs, a new Forty-Sixer ended her quest and led to her fortysixth summit. Champagne was enjoyed by all and meanwhile every possible combination of eleven people with eleven cameras was miraculously achieved. The champagne worked well for upon returning to Uphill there was actually a moment when everyone was talking at the same time. The Glens Falls Chapter is renown not only for its conversation but also its taste in fine champagne! Sunday had indeed turned out sunny and warm with turquoise skies and the views enjoyed along Lake Colden and through Avalanche Pass will never be forgotten. Without a doubt the packs were at their heaviest climbing up through the pass but the downhill roll back to the Loj went quickly and was the end to a great weekend. Oh - and yes, the quotation of the weekend happened that evening at the Noonmark Diner when the intrepid climber and dining companion, after being handed a piece of lemon meringue pie at 10:00 PM on a paper plate, stared and replied: "Did the dishwasher go home?" The only ending for a story like this should be: And they all lived happily ever after.

(Because of the large deposits of iron ore near the

old abandoned mining town of Tahawus many hikers trying to ascend the trailless peaks Cliff and Redfield find that compasses do not work in this area. An intuitive "feel" for the terrain does much better here then conventional navigation. The Department of Environmental Conservation does its best every year to contend with the many hikers and climbers that become lost in the large valley that separates these two high peaks. This outing took place during the weekend of October 28 and 29, 1989. Thanks to my companions Neal (the intrepid climber and dining companion), Darius, Susan, Sherry, Margot, Todd, John, John III, Jim, and Marty, for getting through saturday night's rain as well as the ordeal on Cliff. Our regrets to Mike, the lost hiker, who had to endure several backcountry safety lectures from two DEC Rangers all in the span of about two hours. And a special thanks to Neal for convincing me to keep my mouth shut when I didn't really want to. I doubt if you will ever find Mike lost in the Adirondacks again.)

Gothics and Sawteeth

And there I was once again in that place where nothing made sense and comfort seemed to exist only in my mind and in pictures that I keep hidden. Soon the colors of the landscapes and the birds and the open spaces around me began to run dry. No longer could I recognize the motives of the wind swept sky from the definition of the horizon. The trees and the snow, the sun and the ice, blended together and their very meaning became elusive with every step. The mountains that I had become so dependent upon for spiritual conversation and mental contemplation were in the process of turning their backs on my very soul. Standing on the summit of Basin, halfway through a seven day February snowstorm, I watched in silence as fellow members of my climbing party inched their way toward the apex of this dauntless giant. The hood of my parka flapped loud and endlessly in the abyss of wind pouring over the ridge of this great range. Its noise so piercing that nothing else could be heard above its roar. My mind raced in tightening circles trying to find a reason why these people were compelled to endure this grueling ordeal. This mountain had rejected so many, surely they understood this. The sting of the wind continued biting through my heavy goggles and wisps of ice and snow circling my stance penetrated every unprotected opening. I ground the points of my crampons deep and then deeper into the clear water ice of the summit to ensure a protective hold against the growing force of the gale. The lead rope tight, I waited for the others to advance.

It was a clear sunny day in autumn and my mind was far from the authority of the mountains. Not unlike the calculation of an unexplored approach, the first gaze was one of revelation and wonder. Her eyes radiated the suns reflections like the stars of perfectly cut stones set in flawless sterling settings. Her beautiful face beamed with rays of channeled light like the sun through high clouds at the thunderstorms edge. Her long dark hair surrounded her and reflected the ambient light into a million tiny rainbows. The smile that she gave, like the warmth and beauty of the trilliums in the early spring, led me to gaze into her eyes and be truly captured. As we walked through the forest that day I was to learn just how special she was to be, and every sentence and every smile, was to be a source of wonder and a thirst that I had not known before. The sweet sound of her voice and the image of her face would echo and appear in my mind and in the mountains for many weeks after that day. Her tenderness of character was a river of warmth in which I was compelled to embrace and selfishly bring into my world and to guard to ensure its longevity. She was intuitive and uniquely spiritual. Her understanding of the physical world around her was uncommon and she was not only comfortable, but beautiful in any situation that she found herself in. Indeed this beautiful woman who had come into my life was like the artists palette redefining the colors of life that somehow I had misplaced in these passing years. The magic of life and of love and of being in the mountains was highlighted and reborn through her touch. I could feel the warm touch of her slender hand against my face, caress and then I would kiss it gently.

My fingers became stiff and numb with the freezing stillness of holding the rope against the ice. What in the hell was taking these people so long. If they don't make it to this point soon they can kiss Sawteeth good-by. Can't they see that this big icy rock is forcing them to play its game. It waits for the fearful child and then confronts the lack of self confidence that it possess. At this game it cannot be beaten. I watched with anguish as the climbers below ended their slow ascent and waved a motion that I had come to know all to well. Accepting defeat in the mountains in winter was something that you learned through years of agonizing trial and error. If you were fortunate your errors would not be catastrophic. Emotions here always ran the gamut. A thousand mountains in a thousand snowstorms and still the ice and the sun and the wind control our spirits. Metaphysics and existentialism, they are the root here and are the rules of life and death that the mountains play by. At times our own rules seem foolish in comparison. Year after year it became easier for me to recognize that nature continued to advocate love over gold. It shows up in the most subtle places. She understands these concepts. God how I wish she were with me now.

The Trailless Dixes

(The following is an account of the solo climbing of the five "Dixes"; Macomb, South Dix, East Dix, Hough, and Dix. These five high peaks, rarely climbed in a single day, represent some of the most rugged and remote wilderness areas in upstate New York. Approaching Dix from Hough via the Beckhorn, a false peak protruding from near the summit of Dix, is said by some to be one of the most spectacular alpine ridges in North America.)

As usual my guardian angel kept the weather from turning sour for the weather man had predicted a fifty percent chance for rain. I did carry a pretty good sized pack because I had no idea how difficult the herd paths would be to find and if needed I was prepared to spend a night out in order to get all five peaks. As it turned out while I was packing my day pack the night before it quickly filled up so I ended up dumping everything out onto the living room floor and starting again with the big pack. I got an early start from the Elk Lake parking area at about 6:30 AM. I was kind of uneasy about leaving my car here for any length of time because of all the horror stories involving slashed tires and broken windows that I had heard about. It appeared that many of the property owners in the area did not like the fact that the public trailhead was so close to their property and rumor had it that they didn't mind showing their anger about it. Never the less I began the long trailed hike to Slide Brook and the camp site where I would leave the trail.

The beginning of the trail before the gravel road was just as beautiful as I remember. It was still early dawn and walking through the low pines with the smell of cedar was wonderful and its hard to think of any other way to began any day. It must have rained that night because the trail and the trees were very wet. I dodged water filled pine boughs and jumped puddles and managed to stay pretty dry. Soon the first road cairn was in sight and the hike to the second road cairn went quickly. Hiking on gravel roads has never really been my thing and getting back to the trail was quite a relief. The early morning fall colors illuminated the walk to Slide Brook and at times the dark cloud filled sky made the leaves glow their colors. At times it appeared that the leaves were giving off more light then the sky. Several parts of the trail had tremendous old birch blowdown and in some places the trail was actually quite difficult to find.

To my surprise Slide Brook was indeed a tent city. Several early risers were cooking breakfast and smoke from fireplaces filled the whole surrounding forest. Howling stoves filled the air with a strange drone. As I began the herd path up the brook I noticed a fellow filtering water and we talked briefly. He said that his group of eight were going to try for the Dixes today also. He then asked if I had heard any current weather reports for the day, I said that it might be wise to plan for the worst possible conditions because October could throw anything at you. So far this morning the sun would only peek through small openings in very dark low clouds. These clouds were also moving very fast so while it calm here it could be very different above treeline.

The herd path was pretty well defined up to the point where it starts to go back and forth across the brook. It was just as easy for me to follow the brook up to the first signs of the slide. I did come across a few well placed cairns just before reaching the first slide pitch. The going was arduous for the sand and gravel runoff from the slide was soft and near knee deep. Very difficult climbing. The lower part of the slide did not impress me and I climbed to a point where the cliffs of Macomb's southern summit were in view. When I saw these cliffs I thought to myself how easy this peak would be so I scrambled higher. As it turned out those cliffs were a lot further away then they looked and it took me about an hour of steady climbing to reach them. I probably would have made better time but I could not help turning around and taking in the spectacular views. Tahawus was certainly living up to its name today for it was the only summit hidden by the high clouds. Allen looked awesome standing above all that surrounded it.

Up by the cliffs it is very steep and in some places it was so steep that you couldn't see below from where you had just come from. This may be the only place that I know that is steeper then the Gothics slide. The wind began to pick up and the higher I climbed the stronger it became. By-passing the higher cliffs to the north I continued around them and finally found the ridge. I found the Macomb register at about 9:45. I sat in a protected area near the canister as the clouds became more and more fragmented, and I watched the wind become more violent with every passing minute. There was more sunlight but it could not offset the effects of the winds chill. After eating half of a peanut butter and jelly sandwich I dressed in raingear, to help protect myself from the wind, grabbed my compass and headed east toward the col between Macomb and East Dix.

The path down the backside of Macomb was well defined and it offered some protection from the wind. In coming down there were places where you could see South and East Dix ahead and the pointed peak of Hough to the north. After passing through the col and starting up over the open rocks of South Dix the wind again grew in intensity. At times I had to walk on all fours to keep from being blown over by its force. I knew that the big pack was also making it worse, substantially increasing my silhouette, and the wind pulled and shifted it from side to side. Several times I had to stop my forward progress and lay flat on my stomach and wait for a lull in its force before I could continue. Without a doubt the strongest wind I had ever encountered anywhere. Soon I was near the register on South Dix and the small stunted trees here did offer desperately needed protection from the wind. As I passed a herd path junction of sorts I made a mental note for it headed in the general direction of Hough. Made the summit at 10:30 and rested briefly enjoying the views south and back toward the towering summit of Macomb.

Starting toward East Dix I was accompanied by bright warm sunshine and shortly

I had to stop and take the raingear off. The late morning sun was doing a wonderful job of warming me up. The wind still howled above me but the treed ridge from South to East Dix kept me protected almost the entire distance. Just before reaching the summit of East Dix the network of herd paths becomes confusing because of the terrain mix of wooded areas and open rocks. There is one bad false lead that leads to the north and I followed it for five minutes before it disappeared. I hunted around for awhile and finally found the canister bolted to the east side of a large boulder directly on the summit. As I sat under the big rock the wind made yet another appearance. The views from East Dix, especially to the south and east, are spectacular. I did not stay here long and I had some water and food and quickly started back toward the junction that I had spotted near South Dix. On my way back I passed a married couple en route to East Dix, they were part of the group camping at Slide Brook, and said that they would be happy if they got the three peaks today for they were both exhausted from the Macomb climb. Upon finding the junction I quickly started north down toward the col between the 'hogback' and South Dix. The herd path was reasonably defined and the one steep descent leads you to the camping area on

37

the hogback. The nicely built fireplace and the nicely selected tenting area were a real surprise, such conveniences so far from anything.

The herd path to Hough starts off as easy to follow but the higher you climb the harder it becomes to follow. Halfway to the summit cliffs abound and herd paths go in all directions as the footsteps of countless hikers try and find an easier approach to the summit. The highlight of the day came just below the first bump of Hough. As I was climbing I heard the unmistakable sound of Canada Geese squawking. I turned around to see if I could get a look at them, and from the east flying west were a very large V - formation of probably fifty birds. They were no doubt flying toward Elk Lake. But the new twist here was the fact that I was looking down on them as they flew between Hough and South Dix. Wow, talk about new perspectives on life. At one point they were so close that I felt as if I could have reached out and stole a feather.

Just before reaching the Hough ridge I was stopped dead in my tracks by cliffs. Some of these were just to steep and dangerous to attempt unprotected so I skirted to the west trying to find easier terrain. After some crawling around in the mud I finally worked myself past these obstacles and up onto the ridge. The wind roared as I broke the crest of the ridge and the hike across the summit was noisy to say the least. I found the canister on Hough at 1:30. There is a rock near the summit that protects you from the wind and I sat here and had some food and tried to decide if I was going to attempt Dix or not. I felt pretty good and although I was low on water I had plenty of food to get me through until I was over the summit of Dix. My friends had told me that although the path from Hough to Dix was quite long it did not involve that much elevation. The views from Hough were hypnotic and I hated to leave, the view of Allen is unbelievable. The wind was cooling me down, I had to move.

Going down the north side of Hough is very steep and I moved very slowly. In the col it flattens briefly to a swampy area with much recent blowdown. The blowdown in most cases made the going easier and you could hop from log to log to avoid the bog and swamp below. This still col was especially beautiful and although it was wet and swampy it was a desirable place to behold. Ferns of every type and description were everywhere to be found. Some of the larger varieties were as tall as I was. This place had a prehistoric nature to it. Shortly I began climbing again to what I guessed was the Beckhorn on Dix. At this point I started to slow my pace for I knew that my climbing limit was not far away. I found myself needing rest breaks at closer and closer intervals. My water was low and I knew I had to take it slow and easy. The wind continued to roar above and it grew in force with every step toward the Beckhorn.

The character of Dix Mountain is very different from the other four peaks on this route. As I stood near the Beckhorn looking back toward Hough, and then looking ahead toward the summit of Dix, I realized just how formidable this peak was. In the small alpine col between the Beckhorn and Dix I stopped and put on all of the clothing that I had brought. This clothing included a new gore-tex Peruvian style hat that I had always thought to goofy looking to wear. I was to learn that goofy looking or not those Peruvians knew how to make hats all right. Near the summit I noticed four people huddled on the down wind side of a rock. They looked very much out of place here for only one of them had a day pack, the other three apparently had brought nothing. They left for lower ground as soon as I passed, we waved greetings not wanting to waste energy yelling over the wind. It was 3:30, it had taken me two hours to get from Hough to the summit of Dix. I was beat.

I took many photographs in all directions

from the summit of Dix and the high clouds will make them even more spectacular. The clouds had lifted a bit and even Mt. Marcy was in sight. Views that dominated were that of the Dial - Nipple Top Range, Skylight, the trailless Dixes from where I had come, and of course Allen. The wind was so strong it felt like I was standing alone on some other planet totally isolated from the rest of the world. I could not endure this for long so I quickly began the descent which luckily would be trailed. The long walk down the Dix trail was uneventful and was more like a survival march then anything else. The views toward Elk Lake were wonderful and if I wasn't so exhausted I probably would have stopped and really taken them in. I finally understood Bill Kozel's definition of "test pattern in the mountains", I was so tired I stumbled over nothing and everything. Somehow I had walked right past the lean-to at Slide Brook and didn't even realize it. I did somehow manage to find the benchmark at 2290, but did miss the ones at 2320, 2338, and 2285. The beauty of the Adirondacks seem to make even better sense after a day like this. The warm glow of the autumn leaves, the hospitality of a mountain trail, and the clean breezes cooling my face seem to coax me to stay.

As I walked toward the trailhead, and my

car which contained three bottles of diet coke which hopefully would be used to keep me awake for the return drive, I thought about all that barbecued chicken and scalloped potatoes that I was going to miss at the fall Forty-Sixer meeting. I felt a tad guilty for not volunteering for some trail work this fall but I really needed this climb today. As a matter of fact that meeting was probably being brought to order at this very moment, my watch said 7:00 PM. This is great, I should be hopefully back at the car in a couple of hours. I'll need a headlamp soon, its getting dark fast. Wow, what a beautiful autumn sunset - ha, I got all five today.

I really had mixed emotions when I arrived at the Adirondack Loj for it looked like we were in the middle of a blizzard. The weather prediction was for sunny skies and more moderate temperatures but I really had my doubts. February weather was always unpredictable. Everyone was on time for the 7:30 AM start and the group seemed comfortable and very cordial. Bob, Lynn, and Jack and I had just climbed the Sewards last year so I knew them well. Len and Wendy didn't seem like strangers after their write up in *Peeks* magazine. Brian and I had climbed for several seasons with the Rochester Winter Mountaineering Society and David's name kept popping up in every canister that I opened lately. Tom and Carl were friends of Bobs and although I did not know them at all I felt confident about their participation. Bob made it clear that if the weather didn't change before we reached Rocky Falls we would be turning around. Navigation would be near impossible on the ridge without some visibility. The group was off, blizzard and all. As it would turn out the weather was to be the least of our problems. The walk to the falls went quickly and our first test of the day was to find a place to cross Indian Pass Brook. It was a raging mass of water and huge ice jams lined both banks. Down stream a few hundred yards we found a marginal place to cross, a zig zag pattern across an ice jam. Carl and I stayed down stream even further just in case someone fell in while crossing. We made ready long sticks and ski poles to reach out to anyone who might happen to come down the main channel. The crossing was a bit slow and fearful but luckily uneventful. It continues to amaze me how water at this time of the year can be such a life threatening enemy.

Snowshoe conditions were ideal and soon the group had climbed up through the cliffs and up onto the easterly shoulder of Street. I had never used this approach before, always ascending Street from Nye, and must agree that hiking down the ridge to Nye may be the better way to go. It is quite a distance from the shoulder to the summit and this mile or so brought in some places very deep snow. The lowering tree tops told us that there was not only a lot of snow but the summit was near. David, who had stayed up in the lead trail breaking the entire way, found the canister at about 1:00. When we came upon him he was down on his knees digging the register out of the snow which meant that there was about three or four feet of packed snow under us. The views from Street were superb. This was probably the best view that I had ever had of the MacIntyre Range and Mt. Marcy was framed perfectly between Wright and Algonquin. The isolated snow covered dome of Iroquois Peak looked, from this vantage point, unreachable. David proclaimed that this was his fifth ascent of Street and that in all these winter ascents he had missed Nye every time.

After everyone had stood around and congratulated each other enough to become dangerously cold, the group made the decision to try for Nye. It was questionable at this point as to weather or not we had the time for this. It was about 1:30 and the agreed turn around time would be 3:00 because not only was the snow very deep up on this ridge, but the weather had cleared and with it came frigid temperatures. Bob's thermometer on his backpack said ten below zero.

As many have come to know there is no elegant way to ascend Nye. While still on the summit of Street we took a bearing on Nye, pulled up our hoods, put our heads down and just went for it. The snow laden pines were dense to say the least. One section of the ridge between Street and the bump just to its north is so thick with young spruce its a wonder that more people do not become lost in this area. We must have sounded like a herd of buffalo crashing and branch breaking our way through the dead wood of the dense forest. The clanking of the canister top told me that someone had found the register, I was to learn that once again it was David. He had finally gotten Nye.

Cramming ten people near the Nye register, especially during this time of the year, was near impossible. Everyone took turns standing on the true summit. This may sound simple but imagine ten people wearing ten pairs of snowshoes trying to get around one another in an area about the size of a broom closet. Everyone was very happy that we had made both peaks and the attitude of the group was jovial, even the cold at this point didn't seem to bother anyone.

The group decided to return via the Indian Pass Brook tributary and try to intercept the Old Nye Ski Trail and follow it back to the Rocky Falls red trail. It was about 3:00 and the only questionable part of this plan is that we would have to find a brook crossing at a much wider section downstream. The route would of course not be broken. We figured these things trade offs for not having to reclimb Street and going all the way back to Rocky Falls, essentially backtracking. As we continued down toward the col we picked up what we thought was the right tributary. While on Nye, Bob, Brian, and I had figured solid bearings and followed them without question. Needless to say and for whatever reason, magnetic ore around the summit of Nye or just some sloppy compass work, we followed the wrong drain and halfway down figured out where we were. We found ourselves committed to a steep descent, in the wrong direction, and it was getting very late.

We left the gorge at about 5:30 and knew that we had to at least get to the brook and find a crossing point before dark. Heading due east we walked very quickly as darkness descended we found the brook by sound. It was dark and it was time for a strategy meeting. After breaking out the headlamps and flashlights we decided the plan would be to cross at the closest point from our position follow the brook upstream and try to find the campsite that marked the ski trail junction. It sounded too easy. As we faced the river we could just see the faint outline of Mt. Jo off to the southeast - boy were we off course. If there comes a time when you will be semi-lost, in the dark, in the winter, I was convinced that our time had come.

I remember standing at the brooks edge using my lamp to light the ice as Bob carefully probed the ice for a crossing point. It was pitch black and our headlamps lighted only small circles in front of us. The circular patterns moving back and forth and the dull low frequency of the water rushing under the ice made me very uneasy. Suddenly and without warning Bob crashed through the ice and was splashing and floundering in chest high water. Not to be overdramatic but falling into chest high water under usual circumstances is one thing, but doing so during the winter while wearing a large pack and snowshoes is definitely another. I can still feel the ice cold water splashing in my face from his struggling. Brian, Jack, and I lunged at him with ice axes and ski poles and anything else handy that he could grab onto. He slowly managed to roll over onto his side and crawl back up to the shore. His boots were frozen and his parka and backpack were already beginning to turn white. Everyone in the group had brought plenty of extra clothing and he was literally buried in warm clothing. We quickly took his parka, pack, and snowshoes and banged them against a tree to try and loosen the ice from them. From this point on however we did have to stop several times and warm his feet and change his socks. His feet were not far from frostbite. David showed us a great trick that he had learned in Asia of taking the foot of one person and putting it into the crotch of another person. It sounds kind of funny but it works and brings back a cold foot every time.

Meanwhile the others had found a crossing point. One at a time we all crossed, the sound of the running water under the ice was the only thing that took my attention from the total darkness. Getting everyone across was a major event and we continued hiking quickly upstream. The temperature was dropping and no one wanted to stand around for very long. We must have been a lot further north then anyone had thought because we hiked for over an hour before we found the campsite marker. There were no ski tracks to be found anywhere so we decided to forget the trail and take a bearing almost due south and skirt the western side of Mt. Jo. hopefully picking up the red trail.

Night time orienteering during the winter months is not a joking matter and we all checked our bearings every ten minutes. The fact that most of us were running our lamps on their last set of batteries seemed to give everyone an extra boost of energy. No one was in the mood for a bivouac at this particular moment. We continued snowshoeing for what seemed like hours for the distances at night always seemed infinitely longer. There were several moments when I thought to myself that the trail could be right over there and we wouldn't even know it. Finally it came, Brian called out from the front,"I found the trail - over here, over here!".

Everyone cheered out and the pace quickened as each of us one by one broke out through the brush onto the trail. What a feeling that was, something as simple as knowing exactly where you are. My watch said 9:30.

As we all walked the red trail back toward the Loj the fact that our headlamps were essentially out just didn't seem to matter. Looking off to the west the faint outline of Mt. Jo was outlined by starlight, and soon the lights of the Loj gleamed across Heart Lake acting as a beacon toward safety. The feeling of getting back to the Loj was indescribable, and several of the ADK staff were waiting on the front porch for our return. The warm glow of the Loj fireplace and the hot coffee there was a reward like few others that I had ever had.

In walking back to my car Brian called out , "Hey Jim, we're doing Seymour next weekend, its not broken and they'll be lots of snow, want to come along?" I shook my head, "Sure, call me - preferably not tonight".

(If anyone should find an ice axe in the vicinity of

50

Indian Pass Brook - chances are it belongs to Bob c/o the Albany Chapter of the Adirondack Mountain Club)

Goodby to #2219

The minute I read the news in the newspaper I left work and drove to the church. Standing room only in a very big beautiful church. Big strong men were crying and people were dressed in black suits. People liked you a lot. I know that I will surely miss you old friend. I'll miss those diet cokes stashed away in that red cooler under the seat of your truck. I'll miss those fudge walnut cherry jet fuel what-ever-you-call them cookies that you and Mary used to make. I'll miss that extra quart of water that you always found in the bottom of your pack at just the right time. You know when I first met you I thought you were kidding when you told me that you were coming back from Allen Mt. at 10:00 in the morning. You flipped out your altimeter and said, "Only 2000 more feet to go - have a nice day". I thought you were nuts. Boy could you turn the gas on high.

Do you remember that early morning trail break up Wedge Brook and that snow covered sleeping deer jumping right up out of the trail in front of us. Talk about deer in the headlights. I was scared silly. So was he. The pouring rain on Allen, and you, Neal and I all yelling at each other because we knew it was ridiculous to go any further. And the long faces behind us. You turned and said, "I'm going home", some argued - I knew better. Three feet of snow and pouring rain in December. It was like walking through soggy cream of wheat. Hypothermia 101. Lots of good times. And that fall on Algonquin. When I finally stopped sliding I swung around - the view was breathtaking, the air still and silent. I thought I was finally in heaven. Your hand told me otherwise. Even the bad times were good times.

You were right about this canister business. I remember you saying, "We should really think about it". I was shocked. You were in a different league and I didn't even know it. How could I have overlooked the firestorm of opposition that was to come from the concept of dismantling the summit registers. Maybe the cans should stay but someone's got to do something about the herd paths. I don't know. It's really too bad that this "if they did it - why can't we do it" attitude is strong enough to make people overlook the fact that in environmental conservation, and in life, some of us learn from experiences and often mistakes from our past. You probably knew the way to Allen better then anyone. It's interesting to hear the response from someone who's never been there before. The mess is shocking at best. So goes the relationship between the earth and humankind.

Maybe some day they'll figure out that this debate is about much more then canisters and herd paths to the tops of peaks that were once trailless. This is about the mess that's been created on Street and Nye. Remember that maze of poor camping areas and carved out herd paths created by unsuccessful attempts of Emmons and Couchsachraga from Cold River. The piles of used toilet paper and other visible garbage on Seymour and the East Dix slide. And that entire tree wrapped with orange survey tape on Santanoni so the winter baggers could find it at high tide. The feeling in my stomach watching those people chopping down a field of nodding trillium to set up tents at Blueberry Lean-to was not that great. Maybe someday they'll face those skeletons and crampon marks in the backcountry closet that no one wants to talk about. Some people are careful about their relationship with the environment and some are not. Don't get me started.

The lightning on Haystack - do you remember that awesome lightning on Haystack? No wind, no rain, just fast moving high clouds and lighting that made our ears sting and our teeth buzz. Time for a new Timex. I love that mountain in the heights of summer. A good sweat and if you're lucky a good breeze off Marcy. We did it in three hours once, remember. Now in winter, that's a different story. My toughest snowshoe ever - I was beat. Midwinter and no trail to Haystack. And you were the one who broke the whole way from Slant Rock. To hell with the lightfoots, I loved following those big trappers of yours.

Those old timers, they don't get it do they. How could they. Gore-tex, poly-pro, lithium batteries, sherpas, global navigation systems. The other day my friend Mark called his buddy on the telephone through a radio from the top of Dix! Over and out buddy - oh, by the way could we get a pizza delivered up here. Maybe by air! It's a lot easier to get to these summits then it ever has been, and boy are they getting there. The problem is what do we do once we get there.

You said that it would be easy to argue against it. It's much too easy to say that those 46ers who advocate canister removal and the marking of formal trails have suddenly "gotten religion" or are "denying the rest of us the same experience". Man, this saga is getting old fast. If anyone can guarantee that when my children go into the Adirondacks they will not be awed by the kind of deteriorating conditions that are taking place right now, conditions that many people are accepting as status quo wilderness, I'll take the patches off my daypack and eat them. I might keep the trailwork patch - at least I worked for that one. Until then maybe people should think about joining the 3000 or so other climbers, at last count, who might consider what they can give back to these mountains rather then what they can take. Maybe we should all take a few minutes and reevaluate our relationship with the Adirondacks. We could read some of that bothersome handwriting on the wall like the High Peaks Unit Management Plan, or the recommendations of the Northern Forest Lands Council, or even DEC's list of endangered plant species. Their telling us things that we don't want to hear but maybe we should listen, and learn. I really miss these conversations.

Grace told me that the 46ers hit an all time record for members this year. She said that more people are climbing in the Adirondacks now then probably at any time in history. You should see the letters - unbelievable. I took Gapp's advice and worked the mail for awhile - it told me what I already knew. I don't know how she does it. I don't know how the Adirondacks do it. Why do I fear for those poor mountains. Ha! Take care old friend. Watch for those celestial mountains. We'll be there.

#2729

(Stan, my good friend, passed away suddenly on December 20, 1993. He had ascended the 46 Adirondack high peaks in each of the four seasons. He will be remembered as a warm climbing companion to all who knew him. The mountains and I shall miss him very much.)

Looking south west from near Indian Falls

Near the old Plateau Lean-to site

Coming down from the summit of Mt. Marcy

Treeline on Mt. Marcy

Above treeline

Above treeline

Looking west from Algonquin

Looking east from Algonquin

View from Whiteface Mt.

Algonquin from Wright Peak

Dix from near Colvin

Easter Sunday on Esther

It was a grey mist-filled foggy morning and we started early from the new parking area near the Atmospheric Research Center. Although the air felt cool and damp the group felt good about the day and the fact that it was Easter Sunday gave us each a little something extra to carry with us. From the start the feel of the ground under our feet told us that this was to be a day of special importance, a day of discovery for us all. The morning silence was broken by several in the group laughing at the trailhead sign, "This is not a maintained trail". This appeared to be an attempt by the Department of Environmental Conservation to educate hikers about the seasonal erosion problems. This was however the most popular approach to Esther as well as Whiteface and may at some time require some work.

We continue up the old ski lift route toward Marble Mt. and encountered snow about halfway up. The trail seem to have a good hard pack and even though we had all brought snowshoes we decided to wait and see how far the hardpack would hold us without them. We rested briefly near the top at the small trail sign near several old concrete footings. The temperatures were much warmer then we had anticipated and I was perspiring heavily. After a snack we soon made our way over to the Wilmington Trail and started climbing toward Lookout Mt. All along the ridge on Lookout we continued to look for views but the low clouds and fog would not give up a single hint of any of the surrounding terrain.

As we climbed the snow became deeper and deeper. But even with all the snow everywhere you could still tell that spring was definitely on its way. An occasional rock poking through the snow cover and the tell tale melt pockets around trees trunks where the sun shining on them for longer periods now melted away ring like patterns. My favorite part of the arrival of spring was the fact that the birds were back and we listened to them sing and chirp all the way to Lookouts summit. Of course it wouldn't really be spring if that one big glob of wet snow balancing itself in the sun didn't wait until the exact second you walked under it to decide to fall on you and of course hitting you in the exact manner to wedge itself between you and your pack. There are few sensations in this world that even come close to this.

Reaching the height of land and eventually the junction for the Esther herd path, we noticed right away that spring had not yet reached this far up on the mountain. Snow clung to every tree and branch it could find and the sound of the wind above our heads roared with anger. The main trail still had the remnants of a deep snowshoe troth leading to Whiteface. No doubt several grueling ascents had taken place this last winter. It was close to noon so the group thought this a good place to suit up for the climb to Esther. It was also a good chance to have some food to ensure that we had plenty of reserve energy for the ascent. As we had lunch the quiet was that of winter and the only sound heard was that of the wind and an occasional clump of snow crashing down. Clouds raced across the sky above our heads and looked like something you would see in a science fiction movie using time lapse camera tricks.

From the start the new blowdown was heavy and although the snow was wind compacted enough to walk on top of, the branches and boughs held large quantities of wet loose snow. Even with hats on and hoods up the snows cold embrace could be felt with every step. It was almost like swimming through snow. We tried to follow a faint remnant of a snowshoe trail but it kept fading in and out and we soon learned not to trust it. We stopped about five or ten minutes to check our NW bearing that would hopefully bring us to Lookout's summit. The terrain was very tight spruce and soon I began walking with compass in hand and head down. The group stay very close together. Soon we were within sight of the debris on top of the first summit. Just as the guidebook says Lookout has the remains of wooden buildings scattered about, many with jagged nails and steel rods protruding from their rotting frames. On one of the wooden members someone had scratched the word "Esther". Several pairs of eyes looked toward me as if they were expecting me to say we were finally at our destination. I shook my head and trudged onward up the ridge beyond the small clearing where the debris stood.

Heading now on a more northerly bearing, and trying to stay on the highest point on the ridge, we started to descend the col between Lookout and Esther. Although the map shows the maximum elevation loss in this col is only several hundred feet I still always get a little uneasy when going down knowing that this will have to be "made up for" later in the day when I know I won't feel like it. Near the bottom of the col we left our snowshoes and some left their packs in order to lighten the load for the final climb to Esther. If we were lucky the snow wouldn't soften up too badly while we were away from our snowshoes.

The hike from the col to near the summit of Esther was truly a roller coaster climb and we continued from false peak to false peak is search of the canister. The entire group was wet and tired by this point and the fact that the fog kept visibility almost nil made the situation even worse. The snow became less deep near the summit and near one high spot we found an orange ribbon tied to a tree. I thought we must be near something and as I led to a small clearing I stopped momentarily for a rest. The rest of the group coming up from behind, I turned my head to the left and there, about six inches above the surface of the snow, the can with letters E S T H E R. We had found the summit at 2:00.

Most in the group were very happy and smiles returned to everyone's faces. Food of every type and description was enjoyed and even a few chocolate bunnies were seen. It began to rain lightly and the ground fog became thicker then ever. Views were non-existent. Everyone was soaked wet through to the cores of their day packs. I have never been wetter. Looking around at how happy everyone was it just didn't matter - we had climbed Esther Mt. on Easter Sunday. Something spiritual was happening today and I knew it had something to do with the mountains and the snow and the people. Its hard to recall a more memorable Easter Sunday anywhere.

Early Spring at Uphill

As we all sat under the canopy of the lean-to the morning mist rose off the snow cover and hid everything beyond a fifty foot radius. Faint outlines of tall straight white pines extended into the grey-white fog. The occasional peeping of a chickadee broke the silence. Heavy wet snow hung precariously from the branches of small pine trees, here and there a branch flinging upward as its load of snow dropped to the forest floor.

We knew that leaving the security and dry comfort of the trail would take a while to get used to. Once we started seriously bushwhacking however the workout would be intense enough to heat us up to the point where we could ignore the continuous contact with the snow and wet foliage. It was very wet and ideal hyperthermia conditions, certainly unusual for mid-February.

Everyone began to dress up for the upcoming ordeal. I quickly unpacked my mountains of pile and gore-tex and proceeded to put them on. Caroline, a new young addition to the group of late, beamed with excitement as she finally had a chance to try some of her winter gear that she had collected throughout the past summer. We all joked with Chad, another young college student, about his teal, lime green and, hot pink jumpsuit. "If you didn't bring sunglasses for everyone the least you can do is stay in the rear", mumbled Stan as he started off breaking trail. Wisps of pine boughs shook and swirled in his wake. Luckily I felt good about electing the plastic boots and was confident that even if I became soaked to the skin my feet would stay warm.

At about 9:45 we headed in a generally south-easterly direction toward the headwater of Redfield Brook. Hopefully this would lead us to the col between Skylight and Redfield. The herdpaths are heavily used during the summer months but during this time of the year the whole valley appeared abandoned and lifeless. The many snow drifts that crowded the area looked like giant sculptures and we were forced to zig-zag along the brook bed. We snowshoed through very deep snow in places. The sound of log-skidders off toward the south echoed off the hills and valleys surrounding Allen and Redfield. The warm temperature condensed snow made the snowshoeing easy but with this came very wet bushwhacking and every tree that you would touch would send its load of snow crashing down on you. Within an hour I was completed soaked and knew I would have to keep moving. I felt someone grasping for the thermometer attached to the back of my pack. The temperature was dropping - unusual for early spring. With the summit three hours away I was already questioning our chances for success.

The route that we had chosen through the mist filled valleys was unusually hostile. The fog created by the changing temperatures was low and continued to obscure the normal landmarks that were used to navigate toward Redfield. We came upon a large unfamiliar area of fresh blowdown. Although Stan and I both knew that we were headed in the right general direction we also knew that we were far off the normal approach. Maneuvering the snow covered blowdown in snowshoes was strenuous at best. In some places walking the logs would put you five or six feet above the surface of the snow. The endless tangle of giant trunks and overturned tree roots became a formidable obstacle and our progress slowed dramatically. John, Stan, and I, took turns in the trail breaking of one of the most difficult sections of blowdown I have ever encountered. At one point from the rear Dennis called out, "What's the hold up in front?" I thought to myself how this fellow, who I had just met for the first time today, seemed to fit the pattern for the typical aspiring 111er type. If they could follow someone to all 111 mountains they would just assume do it. God forbid you should ask them to lead or break trail.

Stan turned around, covered from head to toe with snow from breaking, and yelled," If you really want to know what's going on up here Dennis why don't you come on up and help us find Redfield Mountain!"

It was really our third date. Maybe if I was lucky no one would call. During the next hour I received four calls for the hike to Street and Nye that I had listed with the mountain club chapter. I had thoughts about cancelling the trip. I had just met Paula through a dating network in Albany. Given a choice between her company and a snowshoe to these two "winter ruffians of the Adirondacks", there really was no choice. But still, she did enjoy hiking, even in winter. Our second date to Wright Peak went off so perfectly. Shrimp, creamcheese, and bagels - what a lunch! I thought this may work. Besides, this would be her second time on snowshoes not her first. I prayed for a merciful winter day.

After an early breakfast at Steve's Place and a quick drive the five of us were off. There was tons of fresh snow. There were no broken trails or tracks anywhere to be found. It was a fairly cold morning with a constant breeze. The pines looked like giant snow trolls with snow clinging to every branch and bow. They peered down at us almost seeming to laugh at our every step as we trudged up the Street ridge. Luckily one of the members in our group was an aspiring winter climber, out in front, he broke trail and led with a passion that only a person in search of a winter number under 100 would possess. He was followed by two college students bound and determined for 46er recognition. Good for the entire group that these fellows were not to be denied today. I don't think their eyes left the map once. Let me see fourteen degrees, ah west, no east. Its that way guys.

We stayed on the frigid summit of Street for all of about five minutes. I was glad we peeled these oranges. It was so cold our lungs ached and our hoods froze upright. We ate what wasn't too hard and drank what wasn't too frozen. I put a water bottle inside my shirt. That was something that I really wanted to do. I piled another layer of gore-tex over Paula. She said that she was OK but I knew that everyone was ready to move on. One in the group unprepared but there were enough spares to keep him from freezing to death. That won't happen again. Do we follow a bearing or follow the ridge - the vote was the ridge! We were off to Nye, more or less. One funny thing about the deep snow is that when you walk on top of it your face is right up there where all the dense brush and branches normally are. And me without my face shield. We must have sounded like a herd of buffalo crossing the ridge. We only crossed our own tracks twice, a new personal best on Nye for me. The compass like a ballet spun to and fro. What a view of the Macs, look at Marcy right between Wright and Algonquin.

My goodness the sun is out. By now we were all soaked to the skin. I'm on my third pair of glove liners. Yuk! It had warmed up to just above freezing and we were all wet to the core of our daypacks. Thank God for gore-tex. We had to do some serious snow tunneling to get up to the can on Nye. More snow here than on Street. We stayed here about 3 minutes and if you ever come here you'll know why. Paula kept a warm smile throughout, don't ask me how. OK gang it's 3:00, we did'em both, and it will be dark in about a hour and a half. Oh-boy. Our trail breaking winter person was still going strong and broke all the way back down to Indian Pass Brook. Following the brook was tough because there was so much snow. And then of course there's crossing the brook, and us without a member of the Albany chapter. Lights and headlamps were out and on about halfway down. What do you mean do I have my "second set" of fresh batteries? We scared a grazing deer silly. Isn't that the moon over there behind Mt. Jo? Boy did it suddenly get a lot colder or what. It didn't really matter because we were all wearing everything that we had brought anyway.

Few sights are as welcome as those lights of the Adirondack Loj shimmering across the snow covered Heart Lake. And few sensations like a chair, heat, and near dead batteries in winter. It was 7:30, late for winter. We dumped out piles of snow from our packs and gaiters out onto the HPIC floor. They leave the HPIC open late in winter for good reason. My face glowed a warmth that only a winter day in the mountains could provide. Paula's cheeks were rosy red. Her smile was still intact. She looked up and grinned, "I guess that means I'm a 3er - right"? What a woman.

(Paula and I were married a year later in a wonderful ceremony at Chapel Pond.)

Letters

(The following are letters exchanged between the author and Grace Hudowalski)

Dear Jim;
March 8, 1992

      I've owed you a letter for ages - only my excuse is the mail has been simply beyond me. I came back from Boulders with more than 140 letters to answer and in the short time from October 12th on, I also heard from more than twenty who finished the 46 after October 12th. Never have I been so inundated or have we had so many new 46ers. All this plus the "Boulder Report" to write and the various holidays to deal with! Oh well! Now I am getting to some of you 46ers who really should have an acknowledgement.

      First my thanks for replacing the books on Street and Nye this past fall. Second I need to know what you have climbed this past winter so I can get your file updated. We've had some great letters of what has happened "up there" this winter and last week I heard from a Silver Bay woman who has climbed with you this winter and is sold on the Adirondacks. Small wonder I would say!

I know there's a difference of opinion on the winter season but it doesn't bother me much. I had a difficult enough time getting some of those persons on the executive committee to recognize the winter climbers in the first place so the dates that they finally came up with didn't matter much to me, a few hours one way or another. And as you know we have a winter rocker so that those who submit their list of mountains of winter climbs to me get one of the coveted W's after their climbing number, and can purchase the rocker to sew on under their 46er patch.

I am very busy, but enjoyably so, keeping in touch with those climbing in winter. I hope you'll update me on your climbs by the end of the season so I can get out a reasonable account of winter activity. I always enjoy your accounts of climbs. Oh-my! Neil Parker just phoned - he's leading a group to MacNaughton this week. I've yet to hear if its been climbed this winter but it may have been. This past week may have been the Sewards and some of the Dixs, a week ago only Macomb was climbed - heaps of snow!

Best regards and good luck with your

leadership in the mountains. Irene Kruse was so pleased to be asked to go with you. She finally went and did Esther without any problem with a couple of the sisters.

Good Climbing!
Grace

Dear Grace;
March 11, 1992

Such a nice surprise to receive your letter yesterday, it sounds like you are keeping very busy with all those new 46ers and now those winter letters! Your Boulder Report is always fabulous and shows your hard work. It is the best part of the *Peeks* magazine - I always read it first.

As I guess you have heard I have been staying active in the peaks with many hikes and climbs this past autumn and during this winter. It is funny because year after year I keep finding myself returning to those special mountains that hold special memories for me. I don't recall how many times I climbed Street & Nye last year! (on several occasions I didn't even sign). Or Marcy, or Algonquin, or the Dixes, or Seymour, for all that matter. On our latest Street & Nye trip this past January the views from Street were, to say the least, indescribable! We found a cliff somewhere between Rocky Falls and Street and stood there in silence for ten minutes just looking across at the whitened 'Macs' held by a cloudless turquoise sky. Wow - the power of beauty!

It was great to hear from Irene again and with her last letter was a listing of outings that her hiking club was going to attempt this year. A few of the hikes were very aggressive and I wrote her back and gave her some suggestions for some more moderate approaches. I was concerned that several of the mileages listed were quite low, and that approaching Blake from Elk Lake as a day hike was quite a difficult route. This summer a friend of mine, from Oneonta, and I will be planning a Sewards trip and I definitely will invite Irene - that will boost her spirits tremendously.

I'm glad to hear that you heard from Susan Spahr. She is very comfortable in the mountains and I had a feeling that she would begin writing to you of her adventures there. We had a great group that day with members of the Glens Falls Chapter, the Schenectady Chapter, and the Niagara Frontier Chapter. I hope that Susans letter to you was good because the conditions on Algonquin that day were pretty wild! Not uncommon for the Macs as you know. No view, high winds, ice pellets, all the things that make Algonquin in winter a real challenge. (that was the first time I consulted a compass while ascending Algonquin) George Banks was along - he's great company anytime!

Broke the trail to Mt. Colden a few weeks ago with members from the Skidmore College Outing Club. What a wild time it was having along a few people who had never been on snowshoes before - what a place to learn. We kept it safe and conservative and went up and down via Lake Arnold - that trail from the lake I do not like in winter so I stay clear of it. Lots of chickadees eating from our hands at both Marcy Dam and at Avalanche Camps - very quiet and peacefully still above Lake Arnold. No views but - we'll go back!

Thank you for sending along the climbing folder but as I told you in my last letter I really do have no interest in a winter climbing file. I continue to have mixed feelings about those who are organizing and advocating this 'special' recognition. Last year while at a 46er meeting I had the chance to overhear several people talking about how they had marked the trail to Santanoni so that in the winter they could go back and 'find it easily'. Weeks later a friend and I ascended Santanoni and found a sight that even photographs do not explain. The tree that held the canister was almost trampled flat, the canister was lose from being stood on, and the tree was wrapped from roots to tip with orange marker tape. I removed so much tape that I could not hold it in both of my hands. The herd path from four-corners was also heavily marked. The funny part of all this is that when these people finally did climb Santanoni in winter they didn't even need all this for the snow level was well below the level of the can - you didn't even need snowshoes. The sad part of this story is that these same people made a spectacle of themselves unwrapping survey tape at the previous 46er meeting in an effort of showing some kind of support for not marking untrailed peaks. It is even apparent that these people are now publishing stories of their hard earned winter ascents in the 46er magazine and failing to mention the extent of there navigational methods. And now some of these people that I overheard that night are actually directors. Climbing the 46 in winter - it doesn't really mean climbing the 46 in winter, it goes along with the rest of the philosophy established by these same people. Last year on a winter ascent of Allen twelve people, many of them aspiring winter 46ers, followed the trail breaking lead of a party of three. Wonderful!

Becoming a Forty-Sixer was a very important part of my life because it meant being part of something very substantial, something that my father and my grandfather respected, something that I knew represented a wilderness ethic that was without equal. Thank you but the aspirations of the winter group in its present form is not for me.

I have begun a personal goal of climbing the forty-six peaks, recognized as winter ascents by the Adirondack Forty-Sixers, but are technically outside the astronomical limits for the definition of winter. If for record keeping purposes you wish to start 46er#2729 (me) as a Winter 1er please begin with Mt. Marcy, climbed by myself on Saturday December 21, 1991.

Thanks again for your letter - I always enjoy hearing from you. Many times while in the mountains I think of you and speak of you with whoever may accompany me. Remember that if you ever need a book taken up, the timing does not matter, let me know and I will certainly do my best. I think that this spring I may earn my first 46er conservation award! Take care and I hope to be hearing from you soon.

Good Climbing !
Jim

P.S. My son, James A. Poulette III, will begin
writing soon so please keep an eye out for his
first letter !

P.P.S. Winter 1991-1992 Astronomical Limits as
defined by the Schenectady Planetarium and Sky
and Telescope Magazine (for reference only):

     winter begins December 22, 1991 3:54 AM
     winter ends   March 20, 1992   3:48 AM

Dear Jim;
May 3, 1992

     A day like today makes me wish all the
more to be at Boulders. I know the ice went out
just a week ago while L. John was up there
bringing down wood from the parking lot - there's
more to be toted down! But regardless of the

weather and the fact that the ferns haven't started to show their heads, I am looking forward to getting there on May 15th - I need at least a week before the 46er meeting.

I meant to go over your file here - I know you've more than the one winter peak you mentioned in your recent letter! And I'd like to suggest you try and forget those hikers who cause you to fret. There have been so many since we organized the winter who weren't up to snuff, this I know, but I decided long ago that it was best to try to set an example and overlook those who don't play the game fairly. It has been difficult at times, but I do try. I too am appalled at the tying up of the tree on Santanoni with those wretched tapes. When an Albany hiker said he planned to spray the treetops so it could be found in winter I suggested he forget it. If it is covered with snow, so what! This year it wasn't but a couple of guys couldn't find it but a nine-year-old lad did who climbed the mountain after they did. Nor could the same couple - both already 46ers, find the canister on Couchee. That I couldn't believe. But the nine-year-old found it! It can't be the weather although at times it can be pretty tough I know.

You mentioned you'd replace another log if needed. The Boultons put up eight logs last year (and one this winter on Table Top) wrote

Esther needs one. It was your mountain as I recall - it has been mine too! If you feel like doing this will you drop a card, I am enclosing one, to Marilyn Corson and ask her to send it on. I am not sure how much space is left in that log but Esther seems to get a lot of visitors these days. If it is inconvenient then don't worry - I will get a note off to Marilyn shortly and ask her to bring a log to the meeting. Someone there will take it up I'm sure. Trying to catch up on local jobs and also get ready to move to camp. This place is a mess, but by the 15th it should be picked up. I hope that all is well and tell James the third that I look forward to his first letter - he'll get an answer.

Good Climbing!
Grace

Dear Grace;
May 6, 1992

Your letter was such a surprise! So nice to hear from you and thank you for sending the post card addressed to Marilyn - I have sent it along and have told her that whenever she needs a book brought up to let me know. We can go up just about any time.

Spring is finally here and Paula and I have just returned from our ADK adopt-a-lean-to trip to Lillypad Pond. What a beautiful hike that is into the Crane Pond area. Saturday and Sunday last were beautiful, but Saturday night had us both up all night because of the unbelievable lightning and wind storm. We could hear trees crashing down all around our lean-to for most of the night. At times the lightning was so bright that you couldn't keep your eyes open. The raccoons and owls stayed indoors that night! Sunday morning the streams, especially North Brook and Paragon Brook, had swelled to beyond capacity because of all the rain we had gotten that night. I'm glad we had a warm dry lean-to that night.

March 21st I climbed Porter and Cascade to bring my special list to 3er status. Remember that I can only count those winter peaks recognized by the Forty-Sixers as winter ascents but fall outside the technical window for winter. Did George and Suzanne tell you about our unofficial ascent of Porter and Cascade in January? It was a perfect sunny day and the snow covered tree giants kept us company all the way over to Porter. Paula added those two to her list of peaks.

Thank you again for the letter and I hope

you have a wonderful spring. I'll be up to see you at Boulders if that's OK. Hope to hear from you soon.

Good Climbing!
Jim

(The following is a letter from the author addressed to the magazine of the Adirondack Forty-Sixers)

When I read in the latest issue of *Peeks* that the 46ers were looking for some way to celebrate their 46th anniversary in 1994 I was moved to think not only about my own relationship with the Park, but with the future of the club in general.

I remembered my father telling me stories about bushwhacking high peaks with the 46ers of Troy when he was a Boy Scout. I remember my first ascent of Mt Marcy with my dad and my brother and the entire three days of not seeing another soul on the mountain. We camped at Four-Corners lean-to in total solitude. We drank from any stream we chose. I remember my Scout Master teaching me how to use a compass en route to Nye. No herdpaths anywhere! We never did find the summit, but that remains the hiking adventure of my lifetime.

Times change. People change. And if they don't change maybe they should. Time has changed this small group of mountaineers into an organization of thousands of people. People who, understandably, love a good thing and climb for the recognition of becoming a 46er. Sadly however, this love of these mountains is taking its toll on the trails, the peaks, and the very core of the Adirondack wilderness. We don't need to dwell on this we all know that it is happening. Some 46ers work trail maintenance as a means of rationalizing our being there in the first place. It helps both me and the Adirondacks, but let's be real. Trailhead usage grows every year. Seasonal splinter groups within the club are clambering for special recognition. Canisters are popping up on some of the lesser Adirondack peaks. It may be time for the 46ers to make a statement about the future of the High Peaks and the role that they might play in that future.

As a statement of their concern for the protection, future, and wild character of the Adirondacks the 46ers, in a highly visible and organized manner, should simultaneously dismantle and remove the 20 canisters which they placed on the untrailed peaks some 46 years ago.

It would represent one of the most significant conservation projects that the 46ers have ever undertaken and would be consistent with the clubs objectives of environmental protection and education. It is the best that we could do. Lets teach and lead by example, not by the numbers and seasons game of 46er logistics.

Becoming a 46er is a wonderful and challenging achievement. This will not change. The spirit of the 46ers will not change. Climbing and hiking in the Adirondacks is something that will always attract those who aspire to climb the 46 peaks. What will change is the fact that the 46ers will have removed their canisters from these untrailed peaks to remind climbers and users of these wilderness areas that in one way or another these mountains, like our attitudes toward them, will be here long after we are gone.

(The following is a letter of response from the author to a solicitation for information from The LA Group PC, a development company hired by the Adirondack Mountain Club to study the Adirondacks, about identifying existing and potential recreational resources within the Park)

Thank you for your letter of March 15th and for giving me the opportunity to participate in the inventory and identification of the existing and potential recreation locations within the Adirondack State Park. I do especially enjoy hiking in almost all areas of the Adirondacks and look forward to even better conservation related attention and programs within the Park. As a lifetime resident, user, and conservationist of the upstate New York area I hope that I can contribute a level of insight and experience that might not otherwise be available.

It is important that you first understand my position toward the Adirondack Mountain Club. I believe that ADK is a wonderful organization and many of its programs represent a sincere attempt to protect the wild character that once was the Adirondacks. If there is to be a steward and educator on the Adirondack scene ADK is probably the best choice for such a task. Their Adopt-a-Lean-to and Adopt-a-Trail programs are certainly examples of their best work. On the other hand as a critic of ADK's escalating marketing philosophy I have found their recent proposals for resource management, which I hope is not being confused with a club business plan, quite alarming at best. Of these proposals, trailhead facility expansion, the building of new structures on ADK owned property within the park, and the reintroduction of mammal species for tourism and economic reasons, are issues that I am most concerned about. In the past I have always looked to ADK as the icon of Adirondack wilderness ethics and I hope to continue this frame of mind in the future.

What this is all boiling down to is that my views and opinions of what the Adirondacks should or should not become are the views of more of a conservationist then the views of the average user. I do have a deep concern for the future of the park. There are many things that must be done now before conditions reach a point where they will be beyond correction. As an example; internal combustion devices such as motorcycles, snowmobiles, and chainsaws, should not be allowed within wilderness areas or in places where they can molest native wildlife or backcountry users. Bicycles or any other non-motorized machinery should be allowed only on paved or hardened surfaces where their damage can be minimized and their effects on trail users can be eliminated. Trail usage during certain times, like snow melt during the spring and periods following heavy rains or blowdown, should be suspended or restricted to stewards in order to minimize the effects of travel during these especially fragile times. Existing maximum party sizes rules within the wilderness areas should be enforced and a backcountry user/ethics course should be available to anyone who is interested.

Of all of the usage concerns that exist within the Adirondacks the high peak region is probably at the forefront. A plan is needed to shift attention away from the high peaks and utilize other areas of the Park such as the eastern Lake George region, the Santanoni Preserve, the Northville - Lake Placid Trail, or the Pharaoh Lake Wilderness Area. The Adirondack Park Institute has started such a plan with its "Centennial Challenge", a collection of hikes and canoe routes designed to expose people to areas other then the high peaks. This type of progressive thinking is desperately needed within the Park. As you may know there exists a debate with the Adirondack Forty-Sixers, another conservation organization who maintains registers on the twenty untrailed high peaks, as to whether or not those registers should be removed and regular hiking trails marked to their summits. This is controversial at best and will meet with much resistance from both sides. I agree with the removal of the summit registers and the marking of manageable trails. This would be a measure for the conservation of certain fragile areas near those untrailed peaks, such as alpine bogs, meadows, and areas at treeline, at the expense of the bushwhacking and trail breaking experiences of the past.

Your letter asked for me to help identify new types of recreational opportunities that should be developed within the park. I would like to help identify "recreational and conservational" opportunities within the park. I hope that you can appreciate the difference. It is my belief that these two issues, usage and stewardship, must be joined in order for the Adirondack Park to survive any master plan containing higher numbers of facilities, programs, or users. I have several points listed here that I feel are important enough to consider for inclusion in a master plan for the future development of the Park;

1. Removal of the 46er registers that presently occupy the twenty trailless peaks. This would encourage and restrict traffic to manageable trail

systems and lessen the deterioration of those fragile areas near those peaks.

2. Limit or restrict trail usage during certain critical times, such as early spring or periods following heavy rains or blowdown, in order to limit damage by users.

3. Allow bicycles and other non-motorized machinery only to those trail systems that are paved or hardened.

4. Publicize and expand the ADK Adopt-a-Lean-to and Adopt-a-Trail programs to encourage an awareness of and participation in user stewardship.

5. Enforcement of maximum party sizes to evenly distribute the number of users within the Park's hiking, climbing, and camping areas.

6. The redistribution of users into other areas of the park in order to reduce the traffic in the high peaks region.

7. Make available to everyone a backcountry user/ethics course at various locations and times throughout the park.

In the short term, and to address the contents of your letter directly, I would advocate the publicity of shifting backcountry users from the high peaks into those other wilderness areas listed above. These areas have reasonable four season trail systems in place, adequate lean-to sites and camping areas for moderate levels of usage, descent bicycle enthusiast potential, and in the case of the Pharaoh Lake Wilderness Area and northern Washington County, offer a wilderness experience rarely found in the Lake Placid or Keene Valley areas.

Your organization has the potential to do tremendous good for the future of the Adirondacks. This may mean however a delicate compromise or balancing act between the needs of the average user and the needs of the Park itself. The Adirondacks are a priceless and totally defenseless resource and need the best strategy and management skills that we have to ensure its survival. Please feel free to contact me in the future if I can be of any assistance to you in this endeavor.

(The following is a letter from the author dated May 10, 1994 to the Northern Forest Lands Council, a group commissioned by the US Congress to study that area in the states of New York, Vermont, New Hampshire, and Maine, that is being defined as the Northern Forest)

Now that I have had the opportunity to read the Council's draft recommendations "Finding Common Ground", and many of the specifics contained in it's technical appendix, I would like to add the following comments to my earlier letter to the Council dated November 1993. My wife Paula and I are land owners and residents of northern Washington County. Although we technically live outside of the Adirondack blueline we do live within one of the proposed boundaries that would define the Northern Forest.

I would like to thank all the members of the Council for their hard work and individual personal sacrifice in putting together this very comprehensive set of recommendations. Considering the time frame and the available resources for this project the technical backup for these recommendations was a major contribution to what I consider to be the overall success of the Council's presentation.

Please accept this letter as my support for the recommendations as outlined in "Finding Common Ground". I strongly agree with the need for Recommendation 13 and the identification and protection of the biological resources contained in the Northern Forest. However, I do submit comments with regard to the scope, language, and overall direction and tone of Recommendation 13. I feel that it is weak in two important areas.

a) Recommendation 13A should outline, with stronger language, the need for an assessment of the biological diversity of the Northern Forest region. The words "biological inventory" may be the kind of strong language needed to get the point across that we must have a reasonably accurate benchmark now in order to measure any future improvements or deteriorations in the health of the Northern Forest ecosystem.

Biological diversity, or the lack of it, is not fully understood with regard to the health or longevity of species and populations that exist within those ecosystems. A complete biological inventory of the Northern Forest now would compile data that would be helpful to future generations as they continue to assess its value.

New York State is very fortunate to have the National Heritage Program as a tool to measure, document, and track rare or endangered species habitat and populations. We've learned a lot from this program. One of the things that we've learned is that more then one half of our rare or endangered plant species exist in large proportions in the four fastest growing counties in the state. This kind of data has practical applications in evaluating land usage and species protection. This kind of a program on the entire Northern Forest could help prioritize where and when resources should be used for protection or acquisition.

b) Recommendation 13D should outline, with more detail, a stronger direction for research in bio-diversity recognition and conservation. The Council has the ability, the technical backup and expertise, and maybe the obligation to recommend a more specific platform for research.

An example of such a platform might be to model the "Wilderness Recovery Philosophy" and the theory of cores and corridors suggested by Dr. Reed Noss. This could be easily done with the existing cores within the region, that is the

Adirondacks, Greens, Whites, and Longfellow Mountain areas. Obviously this is a long term proposal and will not yield instant gratification. Modeling links between these areas and then studying the traffic and migrations of species within these corridors could help us to better understand if scattered cluster developing and forestry practices, on a large scale, would be feasible.

Thank you for sending me a copy of the Draft Recommendations, making available the technical appendix at the listening session in Queensbury, and for allowing me to comment on both. I look forward to the Council's final report to the Congress and to the governors of the four Northern Forest states.

(The following is a letter from the author dated June 2, 1994 to the NYS Department of Environmental Conservation Regional Forestry Manager with comments on the Initial Draft of the High Peaks Wilderness Complex Unit Management Plan)

Having had the opportunity to review the Initial Draft of the High Peaks Wilderness Complex Unit Management Plan (HPWC UMP) dated January 1994 I would like to submit the following comments. It is my understanding that the Draft will be modified and refined prior to its release for review to the general public and I look forward to the Department's final Plan. As a backcountry steward and user of the high peak region I have felt compelled to offer to you what I hope will be another perspective in view of the changes that the high peak interior has seen in the last several decades.

My comments are directed at: (1) the proposals of the Adirondack Council, and (2) the issue of campfire usage within the interior.

(1) The Adirondack Council has made several recommendations with regard to user access to the interior. I strongly agree with several of these proposals and feel that they are worthy of

reiteration:

(a) Closing of the South Meadow Road, without the addition of any new visitor or parking facilities at the South Meadow - Adirondack Loj Roads junction.

(b) Use ORDA (Olympic Regional Development Authority) visitor facilities already in place at the Van Hoevenburg Intensive Use Area to gradually shift automobile parking and user access away from the Heart Lake area.

(c) Revaluate automobile access to trailheads leading to the interior.

Automobile access to the various trailheads leading to the interior has led to a less then ideal situation in terms of, both the numbers of users entering the HPWC every year, and the mechanical problem of where to park motor vehicles. To quote the Adirondack Council:

"The Department should take steps to discourage the current overuse of the Adirondack Loj Road entranceway to the HPWC, so that the HPWC can eventually recover from the abuses of the past and realize its full potential as a true wilderness resource. Increasing the distance visitors must walk to access the overused wilderness interior is an effective and legitimate way to help realize this goal."

This is a well articulated core concept for the future health of the interior.

While I agree in principle with the Council's statement I do feel that it should be expanded and include stronger language to include other automobile access routes such as the roadways leading to Upper Works, Garden, Ausable Valley, Coreys-Axton, and Elk Lake. Closing the South Meadows Road will certainly push more users into other already overcrowded trailhead facilities and would be a temporary curtailment. A more long range approach may be the establishment of a minimum "set back requirement" for any type of automobile parking facility. Although this concept will certainly bring objections from private land owners, including several local conservation organizations who own facilities adjacent to the HPWC, it may be a viable and necessary proposal for the long term health of the interior.

(2) Campfires. I love campfires. I always have. However, the importance and destructive nature

of campfire usage within the interior continues to be a major contributor to the overall decline of the region's health. Physically it appears to be the most urgent and visible form of the interior deterioration. The compaction of soils and ground cover, scarred trees and vegetation, and safety hazards from careless users are biological situations that cannot be tolerated at any level within the interior.

While I agree with the Department's recommendation to eliminate all fires and fire rings within the Marcy Dam - Lake Colden corridor I feel again that it should be drastically expanded. Closing these areas to fires will inevitably push users into adjacent areas where fires would presumably be permitted. People will walk the extra mile to build a campfire. This may or may not be desirable. To put it somewhat bluntly, playing a shell game with users has not worked in the past and will not work in the future. Popular camping areas such as Uphill, Feldspar, Indian Falls, Ward Brook, Cold River, and Slide Brook would all feel the strain from a partial campfire ban and these areas should be considered and included in any campfire ban evaluation.

Lastly, I read with great pleasure Section II of the Draft entitled "Biophysical Resources" of the HPWC. This is a wonderful compendium of the best that the Adirondacks High Peaks has to offer, not only to the residents of the State of New York, but to mankind as a biological investment in a broad spectrum of plant and animal species. This, coupled with the Department's Natural Heritage Program List of Endangered Species, is a very complete accounting of what we do possess right here in our own back yard. I commend and congratulate the authors.

A 46er Vesper

(The following vesper meditation was written by George Sloan, 46er #2651, and orally delivered to the Annual Fall Adirondack 46er Meeting held on October 10, 1992 in Keene Valley, New York)

1992 marks the centennial of the Adirondack Park. There is much to celebrate this centennial year as the Adirondack Park prepares for its second century.

When the state legislature created the Adirondack State Park in 1892, much of the region had been reduced to a cemetery of charred stumps and mudflats, a depressed landscape ravaged by 50 years of logging. By 1892, only about five percent of the original timber remained. Today, thanks in large part to the foresight of the creators of the park, the forests have largely grown back and much of the original wildlife has returned, either on its own, or through restoration efforts.

But will there be a bicentennial? The fact that there has been an Adirondack Park for 100 years does not guarantee that there will be one for another 100. The questions that surrounded the creation of the park 100 years ago - questions of land use, development, and wilderness preservation - are still being debated. And in recent years, there has been more and more proposals to weaken the parks current constitutional protection.

Throughout history we have seen that when the economy falters, that which is perceived to be a luxury, even if it isn't, is the first to be offered up for sacrifice. Is the Adirondack Park such a luxury?

The Park is a patchwork of public and private lands. Its 6 million acres encompass an area as large as the state of Vermont. It is the size of Yellowstone, Yosemite, Grand Canyon, Glacier, and the Great Smoky Mountain national parks combined. Its seems humanly impossible to manage, and nobodies quite sure if it really is a park.

This mix of public and private lands, which makes the Adirondack Park so special and unique, is also what has created such a dilemma for the park. On the one hand, continued economic growth threatens the environmental stability of the public portions of the park. But, on the other hand, the park system we've developed requires constant acceleration to avoid unemployment, and hardship for the private portions.

It's a trap. But there have to be ways to step out of this trap. A society that can develop solar powered calculators must have the brain power to balance these seemingly disparate interests.

Those of us who have been hiking in the Adirondacks for a number of years have personally witnessed just a small sampling of the stresses which are being imposed on the Adirondack wilderness. We have all seen changes such as trail erosion, herd paths that look like well worn trails, new erroneous herd paths in places, increased use in areas where you seldom saw other people, survey tape constantly found on trailless peaks. All of these represent serious threats to the character of the region.

The Adirondacks give us a sense of place, roots and familiarity. Author Bill McKibben, himself an Adirondack Park resident, provides us with a possible viewpoint on which to base difficult decisions that will determine the future of the Adirondack Park in his recent book, The Age of Missing Information. He says:

"Human beings - any one of us, and our species as a whole - are not all important, not at the center of the world. That is one essential piece of information, the one great secret, offered by any encounter with the woods or the mountains or the ocean or any wilderness or chunk of nature or patch of night sky. I can sit on the knob above the pond and see the hills stretch off into the blue-gray distance; I can hide myself quietly on the edge of a glade and watch the deer and the chipmunks and the bugs and the flowers and the old tree rotting; I can lie on my back and watch the vultures circle - and I would be a fool to think that this had anything to do with me, to think that it wasn't here long before me, or that it didn't exist for its own reasons, quite independent for my need for beauty or "solitude". It's true that if I wanted to I could destroy it - set fire to it, or develop a ski resort. And we as a species have the power, by forever putting ourselves first, to end it forever with our weapons, or damage it terribly by changing the climate or eroding the ozone or altering the other fundamental systems on which it depends. We have the power to make the world fit our people-centered vision. But that obviously doesn't mean, wouldn't mean, that this view of the world was correct. Some environmentalists have begun talking about "deep ecology" in recent years - about the idea that we must see the earth as a whole, and that if we insist on dominating everything, we'll create for ourselves an unlivable

115

world. But the vital idea comes best from the encounter with the real world - the real world, the one that was here before us."

Will there be an Adirondack Park bicentennial for future 46ers to celebrate? If so, what kind of park will they be celebrating? The answer to those questions is, "It's up to us: it's up to us."

Ethics and Being There

Climbing and hiking the high peaks in New York State's Adirondack Park can be the adventure of a lifetime. With this adventure however comes an inevitable risk and need for proper preparation as well as a responsibility to the biological sensitivity of the area. Persons entering the interior of the high peak region should prepare for dramatic changes in weather and the need for an emergency bivouac should conditions prove necessary. Snow has been experienced in the higher elevations during every month of the year. Synthetic fabrics rather then clothing made from natural materials are highly preferred not only for its ability to stay warm when wet but also for its protection from the wind. Synthetic clothing is also lighter, easier to pack, and dry in a fraction of the time needed by natural fibers like cotton or wool. Learn to identify hyperthermia and heat exhaustion and how to avoid them. Potable water does not exist in the Adirondack Park and every precaution should be taken to purify water by boiling, chemical purification, or filtration. Sign in as well as out at all DEC trailhead registers. In the event of a search - these registers are your best bet of being found. Always leave word with a relative or friend of your trips itinerary and timetable when going into the Parks interior. Every year hundreds of people become lost in the Adirondack State Park. No one plans on being lost. Most are found, some are not.

Backcountry ethics has become a buzz work, but it is real, and it is a responsibility of all high peak interior users. Learn about protected and endangered species of plants and animals that exist within the park and watch for them. Keep to the trails in order to protect side vegetation and minimize erosion. Talk with rangers and stewards about how you can do your share to use the trails and alpine summit areas properly. Educate yourself about the needs of the Adirondacks and specifically the needs of the fragile alpine zones that exist above the treeline. When above treeline stay on the rocks. One careless step can destroy a whole miniature community of alpine plant life. Take care not to molest or disturb native wildlife. If you come across a bear or a deer or a bobcat give them space and a chance to move on quietly. Nuisance wildlife, or wildlife that has been imprinted with human presence and behavior, exists in all parts of the Adirondacks. Such animals, like black bears, can be dangerous. The safest method to avoid such encounters is to keep food sealed and out of reach. Bears don't want what they can't smell. Hanging from a line suspended between two trees works as long as it's well constructed. This works well, however on one occasion at Lake Arnold a hungry black bear sat under the food bag all night and cried from dusk to dawn. Remember where you are and by all means use common sense. Remember this one; "If you carry it in, carry it out". This adage could never be said enough You wouldn't want people throwing trash in your living room would you?

Those who plan to climb the untrailed Adirondack high peaks have a special obligation to take extra care with regard to those who may be asked to search for them. This is especially true for winter mountaineers. Climbing these peaks with a strong party, parties of four or more experienced individuals, is strongly recommended. The winter season as well as the winter fringe season, late autumn and early spring, call for a greater degree of preparedness in these trailless areas. Specialized equipment is required during winter and signs have been posted at most trailheads requiring snowshoes and/or skis during winter months.

If you are interested in volunteering some time as a backcountry steward, working in the areas of trail maintenance or summit restoration, or just wish to learn more about how you can safely use the Adirondacks High Peak Region, contact the Adirondack Forty-Sixers or the Adirondack Mountain Club.

If you are interested in more information about the Adirondack State Park or the Adirondack High Peak Region, the following is a list of suggested sources where trail guides, books, maps, and other safety and conservation related information can be gathered;

Trailmasters
The Adirondack Forty-Sixers
RD1, Box 390
Morrisonville, New York 12962

The Adirondack Mountain Club
Trails Program
RR #3, Box 3055
Lake George, New York 12845-9523

The Lake Placid Chamber of Commerce
Main Street
Lake Placid, New York 12946

NYS Department of Environmental Conservation
Division of Lands and Forests
50 Wolf Road
Albany, New York   12233

Adirondack Council
Church Street, PO Box D-2
Elizabethtown, New York   12932-0640

Hebron Conservancy
RR3 Box 3158
Salem, New York 12865

About the Author

Jim Poulette was born in Troy, New York. He was introduced to backpacking at an early age by his father and has been hiking and climbing in the Adirondack Mountains for over 25 years. He is a wildlife rehabilitator licensed by the New York State Department of Environmental Conservation and the United States Department of the Interior. He is an active member of the Adirondack Council, Adirondack Forty-Sixers, and participates in the Adopt-a-Lean-to program sponsored by the Adirondack Mountain Club and DEC. He is a licensed Adirondack Guide, President and founding organizer of the Hebron Conservancy, and a lobbyist for land and easement acquisition and protection within the Park. Jim and his wife Paula reside in Hebron, New York where they own and maintain a small wildlife rehab facility and sanctuary. This is his first book.

All photographs were taken by the author using Kodak Tri-X Pan 35mm black & white film.

The author feels, as someone who loves and respects the Adirondacks, that he shares in the responsibility to acknowledge that these lands were once under the stewardship of, and inhabited by, *aboriginal peoples. This is not the forum for a discussion about the state of those peoples or the condition of these lands.*

To all of the aboriginal peoples of the Adirondacks,

Best Wishes, In Peace.